Collections for Young Scholars™

EXPLORING SOUNDS AND LETTERS

KINDERGARTEN

PROGRAM AUTHORS

Marilyn Jager Adams

Carl Bereiter

Jan Hirshberg

Valerie Anderson

Robbie Case

CONSULTING AUTHORS

Michael Pressley

Marsha Roit

Iva Carruthers

Bill Pinkney

OPEN COURT PUBLISHING COMPANY

Cover art by Shirley Beckes
Interior art by Shirley Beckes and Jack Wallen

20 19 18 17

Letter Recognition

Directions: Find and circle small letters *a, b, c, d, e, f,* and *g.*

Copyright ©1995 Open Court Publishing Company

Exploring Sounds and Letters

Directions: Write small letters *a–h* under the matching capital letters.

Forming Letters

Directions: Draw a line from the capital letter to its matching small letter.

Lesson 16

A	c	e	a
E	e	h	l
I	j	i	l
O	c	o	e
U	v	w	u

Directions: Circle the small letter that matches the capital letter.

Letter Recognition

Lesson 18

Directions: Complete the capital and small forms of the letters Ll, Mm, and Nn.

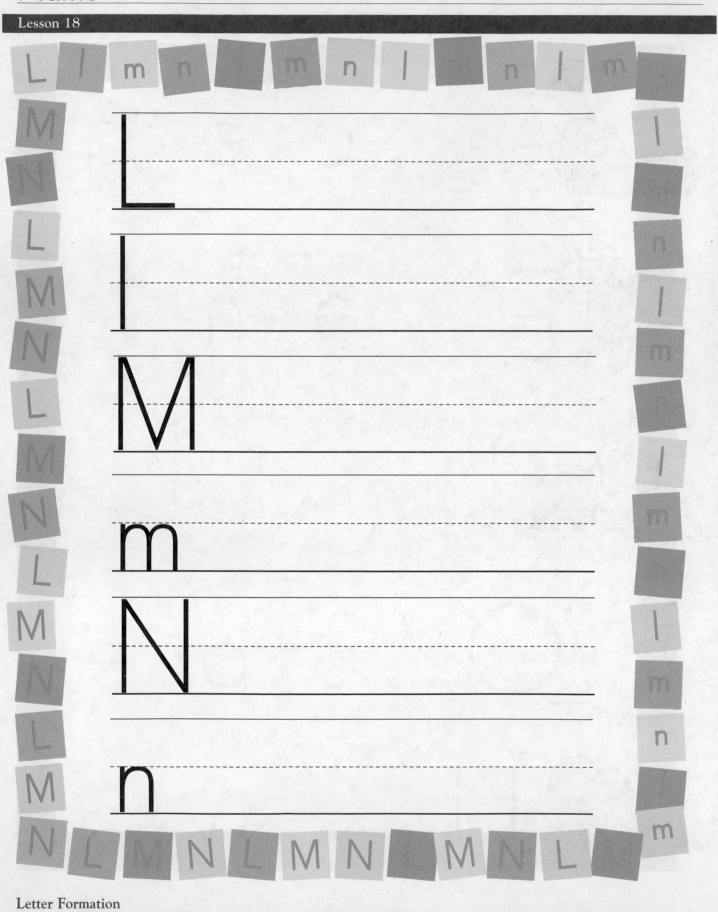

Exploring Sounds and Letters

Copyright ©1995 Open Court Publishing Company

Name

Directions: Connect the dots, in order from A to N, to complete the picture of the bluebird.

Alphabetical Order

Exploring Sounds and Letters

9

Directions: Connect the capital letters from *I* to *O* to help the chef reach the pot at the end of the maze.

Alphabetical Order

Exploring Sounds and Letters

Directions: Circle each capital letter and draw a line to its matching small letter.

Letter Recognition

Name

Ss

Tt

Directions: Write the capital and small forms of the letters Ss and Tt and color the flower petals that match the letter in the center of each flower.

Letter Recognition

12

Exploring Sounds and Letters

Uu

Vv

Letter Recognition

Directions: Circle each capital letter and draw a line to its small form.

Copyright ©1995 Open Court Publishing Company

Letter Recognition

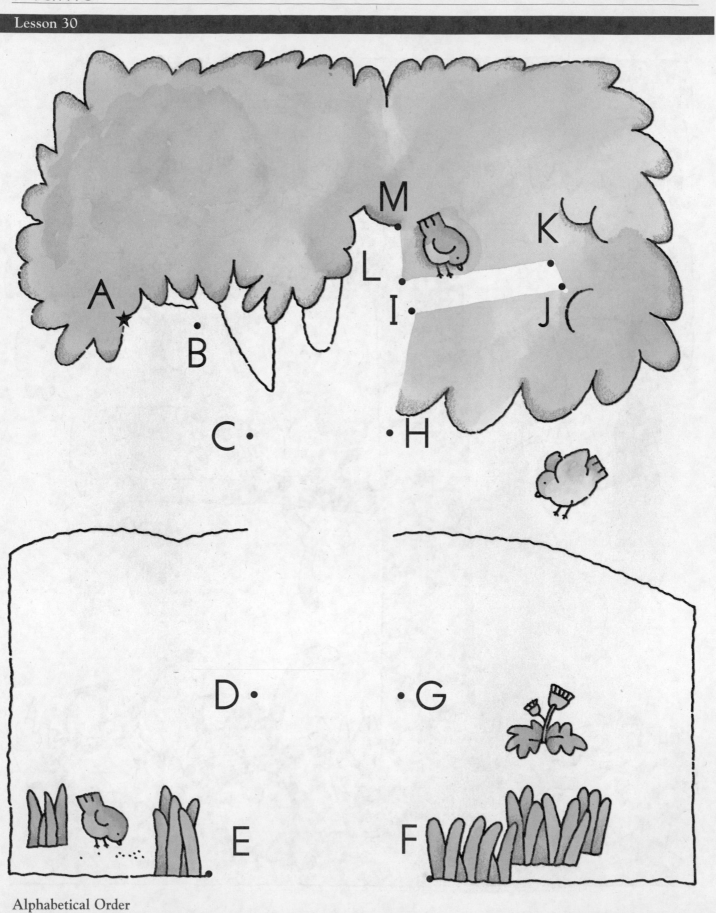

Directions: Connect the dots, in order, from A to M, to complete the picture of the elm tree.

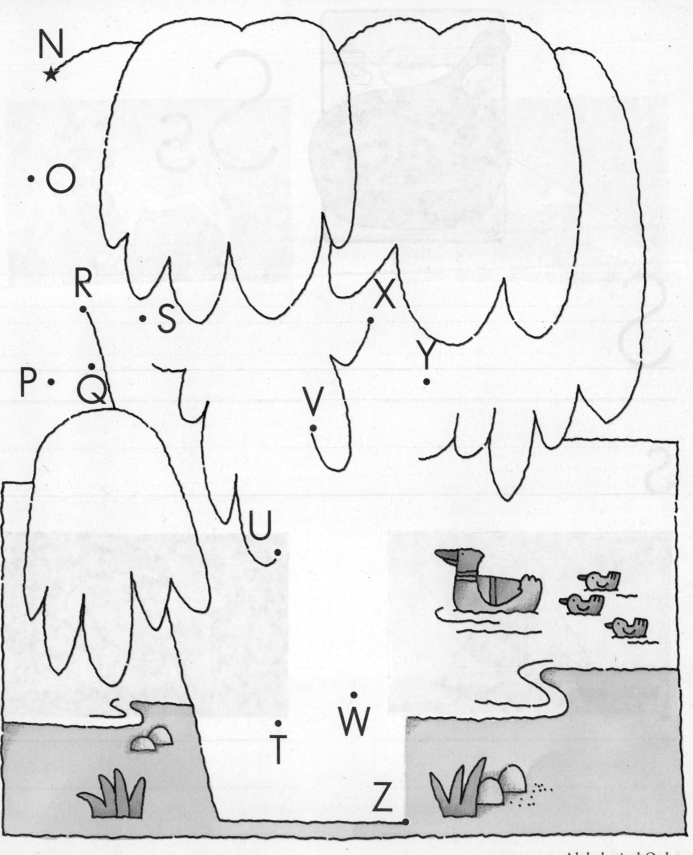

Directions: Connect the dots, in order, from N to Z, to complete the picture of the weeping willow tree.

Alphabetical Order

Directions: Write the letter s under the picture whose name ends with the sound of s.

S s

S

s

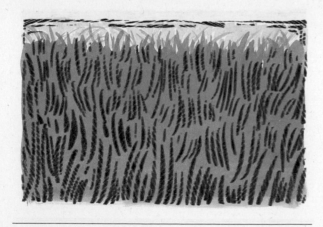

Copyright ©1995 Open Court Publishing Company

Directions: Write the letter m under the picture whose name begins with the sound of m.

Mm

M

m

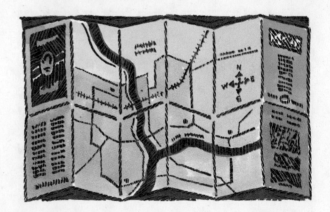

Copyright ©1995 Open Court Publishing Company

_____

- - - - - - - - - - - - - - - - - -

_____

Directions: Write the letter m under each picture whose name begins with the sound of m.

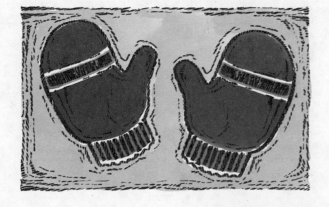

_____

- - - - - - - - - - - - - - - - - -

_____

Matching Sounds and Letters

Directions: Write the letter m under the picture whose name ends with the sound of m.

Mm

M

m

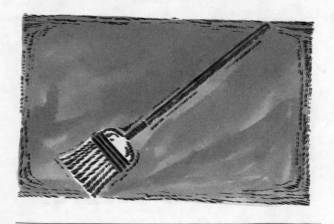

Directions: Write s under each picture whose name begins with the sound of s, and write m under each picture whose name begins with the sound of m.

Matching Sounds and Letters

Exploring Sounds and Letters

Directions: Write *s* under each picture whose name begins with the sound of *s*, and write *m* under each picture whose name begins with the sound of *m*.

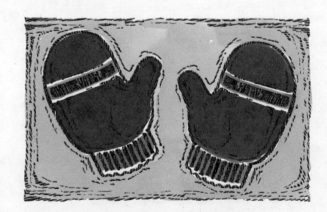

Matching Sounds and Letters

Name

Dd

D

d

Directions: Write the letter d under the picture whose name begins with the sound of d.

Matching Sounds and Letters

Exploring Sounds and Letters

Name

Lesson 37

Matching Sounds and Letters

Exploring Sounds and Letters

Copyright © 1995 Open Court Publishing Company   Directions: Write the letter *d* under each picture whose name begins with the sound of *d*.

Directions: Write the letter *d* under the picture whose name ends with the sound of *d*.

Dd

D

d

Matching Sounds and Letters

Exploring Sounds and Letters

Lesson 38

Matching Sounds and Letters

Directions: Write m, d, or s next to each picture whose name ends with the sound of m, d, or s to complete the word.

brea

dru

bu

ha _____

ga _____

be _____

Matching Sounds and Letters

P p

Directions: Write the letter p under the picture whose name begins with the sound of p.

P

p

Matching Sounds and Letters

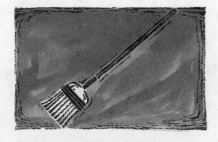

Directions: Write the letter p under each picture whose name ends with the sound of p, and write m under each picture whose name ends with the sound of m.

Copyright ©1995 Open Court Publishing Company

Matching Sounds and Letters

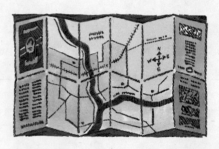

Directions: Write the letter *p* under each picture whose name ends with the sound of *p*, and write *m* under each picture whose name ends with the sound of *m*.

Matching Sounds and Letters

Directions: Write the letter t under the picture whose name begins with the sound of t.

T t

T

t

Matching Sounds and Letters

Exploring Sounds and Letters

Directions: Write the letter *t* under each picture whose name begins with the sound of *t*.

Matching Sounds and Letters

Directions: Write the letter t under the picture whose name ends with the sound of t.

T t

T

t

Exploring Sounds and Letters

Matching Sounds and Letters

Name _____

Directions: Write the letter *h* under the picture whose name begins with the sound of *h*.

Hh

H

h

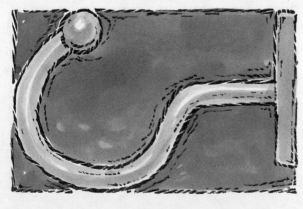

_____

- - - - - - - - - - - - - -

_____

_____

- - - - - - - - - - - - - -

_____

Matching Sounds and Letters

Exploring Sounds and Letters

Directions: Write the letter *h* under each picture whose name begins with the sound of *h*.

Matching Sounds and Letters

Directions: Write the letter a under the picture whose name has the sound of short a in it.

A

a

Matching Sounds and Letters

Exploring Sounds and Letters

Lesson 45

Directions: Write the letter *a* under each picture whose name has the sound of short *a* in it.

Matching Sounds and Letters

Exploring Sounds and Letters

bat   cat

hat   pat

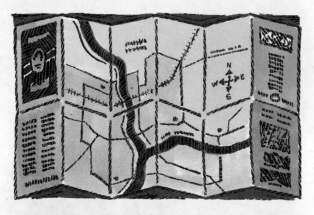

sap   map

sad   pad

Directions: Circle the word with the sound of short *a* that names the picture.

Copyright ©1995 Open Court Publishing Company

Matching Sounds and Letters

Exploring Sounds and Letters

Lesson 47

can   cap

hat   ham

ram   jam

man   fan

Copyright © 1995 Open Court Publishing Company

Directions: Circle the word with the sound of short a that names the picture.

Matching Sounds and Letters

Directions: Circle the word that names the picture.

lock   rock

mop   tot

hot   fox

pot   drop

Matching Sounds and Letters

Copyright ©1995 Open Court Publishing Company

Exploring Sounds and Letters

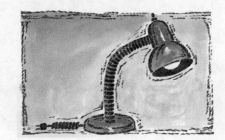

Matching Sounds and Letters

Directions: Write the letter a under the picture whose name has the sound of short a.

Matching Sounds and Letters

Exploring Sounds and Letters

Directions: Write the letter *a* under each picture whose name has the sound of short *a*.

Matching Sounds and Letters

Lesson 52

Directions: Write the letter *b* under the picture whose name begins with the sound of *b*.

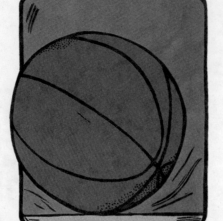

Bb

B

b

Matching Sounds and Letters

Copyright ©1995 Open Court Publishing Company

Exploring Sounds and Letters

_____

- - - - - - - - - - - - - - - - -

_____

_____

- - - - - - - - - - - - - - - - -

_____

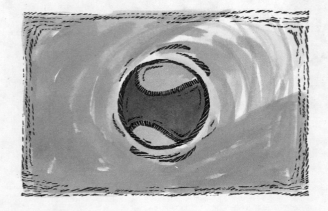

_____

- - - - - - - - - - - - - - - - -

_____

_____

- - - - - - - - - - - - - - - - -

_____

Matching Sounds and Letters

Directions: Circle all the pictures that begin with the sound of b.

Copyright ©1995 Open Court Publishing Company

Matching Sounds and Letters

Exploring Sounds and Letters

Cc

Directions: Circle all the pictures that begin with the sound of *b*.

C

C

_____

\- \- \- \- \- \- \- \- \- \- \- \- \- \- \- \- \- \-

_____

_____

\- \- \- \- \- \- \- \- \- \- \- \- \- \- \- \- \- \-

_____

_____

\- \- \- \- \- \- \- \- \- \- \- \- \- \- \- \- \- \-

_____

_____

\- \- \- \- \- \- \- \- \- \- \- \- \- \- \- \- \- \-

_____

Matching Sounds and Letters

Directions: Follow the maze and circle each stone with a picture whose name begins with the sound of c (/k/) to help the Prince find his castle.

Matching Sounds and Letters

Exploring Sounds and Letters

Directions: Follow the maze and circle each stone with a picture whose name begins with the sound of *c* /k/) to help the Prince find his crown.

Matching Sounds and Letters

Directions: Write the letter d under the picture whose name begins with the sound of d.

Dd

D

d

Lesson 56

Directions: Write the letter d under each picture whose name begins with the sound of d.

Matching Sounds and Letters

Exploring Sounds and Letters

Directions: Write the letter e under the picture whose name has the sound of short e.

Ee

E

e

Matching Sounds and Letters

Exploring Sounds and Letters

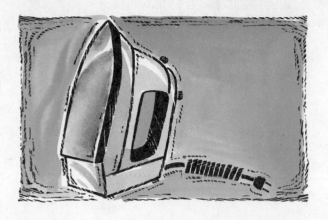

Matching Sounds and Letters

Lesson 59

Directions: Write the letter *f* under the picture whose name begins with the sound of *f*.

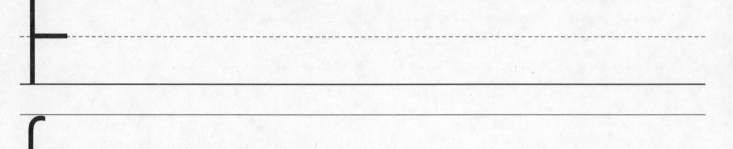

F

f

Matching Sounds and Letters

Exploring Sounds and Letters

Matching Sounds and Letters

Matching Sounds and Letters

Exploring Sounds and Letters

Matching Sounds and Letters

Name _____

Gg

G _____

g _____

_____   _____

- - - - - - - - - - - -   - - - - - - - - - - - -

_____   _____

Directions: Write the letter g under the picture whose name begins with the sound of g.

Matching Sounds and Letters

Exploring Sounds and Letters

Lesson 61

Directions: Write the letter g under each picture whose name begins with the sound of g.

Matching Sounds and Letters

Name

Hh

Directions: Write the letter *h* under the picture whose name begins with the sound of *h*.

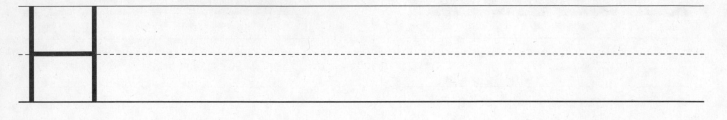

H

h

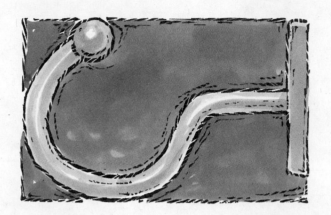

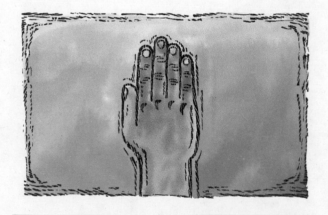

Matching Sounds and Letters

Lesson 63

Directions: Write the letter *i* under the picture whose name has the sound of short *i*.

I i

I

i

Matching Sounds and Letters

Exploring Sounds and Letters

Directions: Write the letter i under each picture whose name has the sound of short i.

Matching Sounds and Letters

J j

Directions: Write the letter j under the picture whose name begins with the sound of j.

J
_ _ _ _ _ _ _ _ _
J

j
_ _ _ _ _ _ _ _ _
j

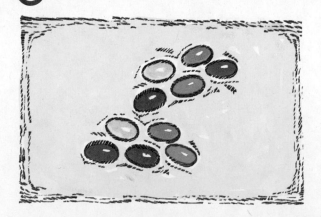

Lesson 65

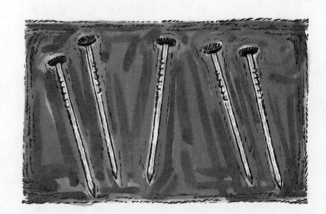

Directions: Write the letter *j* under each picture whose name begins with the sound of *j*.

Matching Sounds and Letters

Exploring Sounds and Letters

Kk

Directions: Write the letter k under the picture whose name begins with the sound of k.

K

k

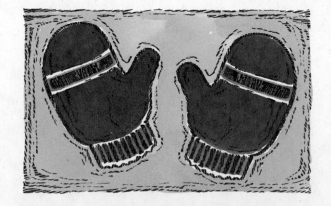

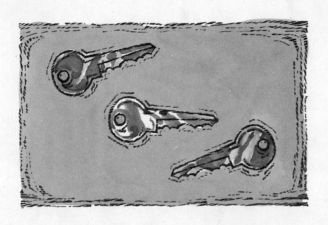

Matching Sounds and Letters

Name

Directions: Write the letter *l* under the picture whose name begins with the sound of L.

Matching Sounds and Letters

Exploring Sounds and Letters

Copyright ©1995 Open Court Publishing Company

Directions: Write the letter *l* under each picture whose name begins with the sound of *l*.

Matching Sounds and Letters

Directions: Find and circle all the objects in the picture that end with the sound of l.

Matching Sounds and Letters

Exploring Sounds and Letters

Directions: Find and circle all the objects in the picture that end with the sound of l.

Directions: Write the letter m under the picture whose name begins with the sound of m.

Mm

M
_____

m
_____

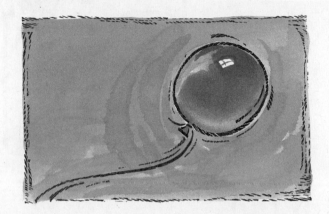

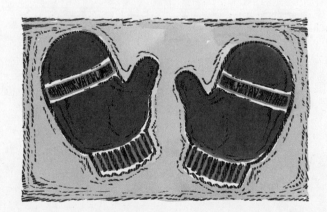

Matching Sounds and Letters

Mm _____

Nn _____

Directions: Write the letter n under the picture whose name begins with the sound of n and write m under the picture whose name begins with the sound of m.

Matching Sounds and Letters

Exploring Sounds and Letters

Name

Lesson 71

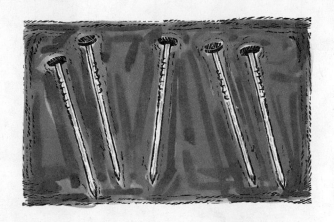

Directions: Write the letter *n* under the picture whose name begins with the sound of *n* and write *m* under each picture whose name begins with the sound of *m*.

Matching Sounds and Letters

Directions: Circle all the items in the cart that end with the sound of n.

Copyright ©1995 Open Court Publishing Company

Matching Sounds and Letters

Exploring Sounds and Letters

Matching Sounds and Letters

Directions: Write the letter *p* under the picture whose name begins with the sound of *p*.

P p

P

p

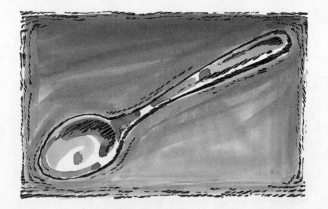

Matching Sounds and Letters

Exploring Sounds and Letters

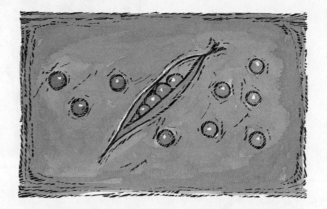

Matching Sounds and Letters

Directions: Write the letter q under the picture whose name begins with the sound of q.

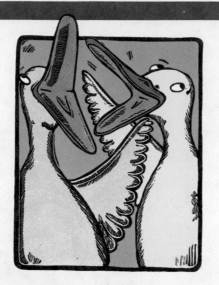

Q q

Q

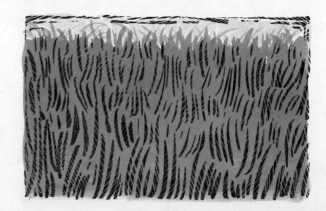

Lesson 76

Directions: Write the letter *q* under each picture whose name begins with the sound of *q*.

Matching Sounds and Letters

Exploring Sounds and Letters

Directions: Write the letter r under the picture whose name begins with the sound of r.

Rr

R

r

Exploring Sounds and Letters

Matching Sounds and Letters

Directions: Write the letter s under the picture whose name begins with the sound of s.

Ss

S

s

Exploring Sounds and Letters

Directions: Write the letter s under each picture whose name begins with the sound of s.

Matching Sounds and Letters

Exploring Sounds and Letters

Directions: Write a capital T under the picture whose name begins with the sound of t.

T t

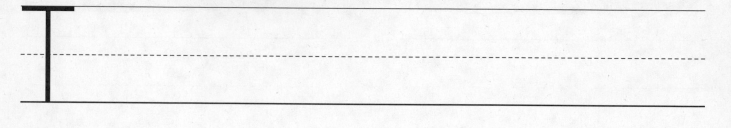

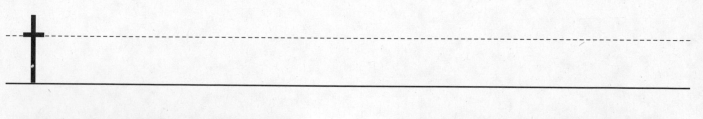

Matching Sounds and Letters

Exploring Sounds and Letters

Directions: Write a capital *T* under each picture whose name begins with the sound of *t* and write a small *t* under the picture that ends with the sound of *t*.

Lesson 81

Directions: Write the letter *u* under the picture whose name has the sound of short *u* in it.

U u

U

u

Matching Sounds and Letters

Exploring Sounds and Letters

Directions: Write the letter *u* under each picture whose name has the sound of short *u* in it.

Matching Sounds and Letters

Directions: Write the letter v under the picture whose name begins with the sound of v.

V v

V

v

Copyright ©1995 Open Court Publishing Company

Matching Sounds and Letters

Exploring Sounds and Letters

Matching Sounds and Letters

Directions: Write the letter *w* under the picture whose name begins with the sound of *w*.

W

W

Exploring Sounds and Letters

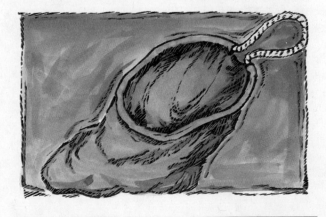

Directions: Write the letter *w* under each picture whose name begins with the sound of *w*.

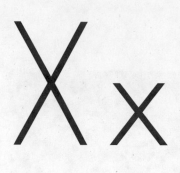

Directions: Write the letter x under the picture whose name ends with the sound of x.

Matching Sounds and Letters

Exploring Sounds and Letters

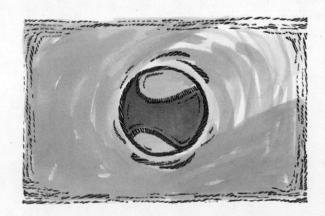

Directions: Write the letter x under each pictures whose name ends withe the sound of x.

Matching Sounds and Letters

Exploring Sounds and Letters

Name _____

Y y

Y

y

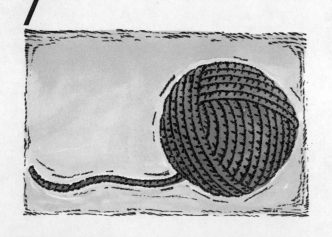

Directions: Write the letter y under the picture whose name begins with the sound of y.

Matching Sounds and Letters

Exploring Sounds and Letters

Matching Sounds and Letters

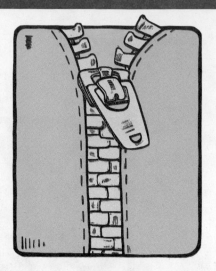

Z z

z

z

Directions: Write the letter z under the picture whose name begins with the sound of z.

Matching Sounds and Letters

Name

Directions: Choose your own letters to write.

Writing Letters

Exploring Sounds and Letters